TOOLS FOR CAREGIVERS

- **F&P LEVEL:** C
- **WORD COUNT:** 35

- **CURRICULUM CONNECTIONS:** community, nature

Skills to Teach

- **HIGH-FREQUENCY WORDS:** a, are, eat, for, go, in, let's, on, see, the, they, to, we
- **CONTENT WORDS:** basket, fill, grow, orchard, pick, ride, rows, tractor, trees, yum
- **PUNCTUATION:** exclamation points, periods
- **WORD STUDY:** long /e/, spelled ea (eat); long /e/, spelled ee (see, trees); long /o/, spelled ow (grow, rows)
- **TEXT TYPE:** factual description

Before Reading Activities

- Read the title and give a simple statement of the main idea.
- Have students "walk" though the book and talk about what they see in the pictures.
- Introduce new vocabulary by having students predict the first letter and locate the word in the text.
- Discuss any unfamiliar concepts that are in the text.

After Reading Activities

Explain to readers that apples grow in fall. Talk about things students may do in fall, such as trick-or-treat, visit an apple orchard or pumpkin patch, or carve a pumpkin. Spark thoughts about other items we see in fall. Then ask readers to draw some and write out what each item is under their drawings. Ask them to share their fall items with the class.

Tadpole Books are published by Jump!, 5357 Penn Avenue South, Minneapolis, MN 55419, www.jumplibrary.com

Editor: Jenna Gleisner **Designer:** Michelle Sonnek
Photo Credits: Thomas Filke/Shutterstock, cover (background); Hurst Photo/Shutterstock, cover (foreground); Africa Studio/Shutterstock, 1; Karen Christensen/Shutterstock, 2br; Tatevosian Yana/Shutterstock, 2tr, 3; JP Chretien/Shutterstock, 2mr, 4–5; Artur Synenko/Shutterstock, 6–7; hanapon1002/Shutterstock, 2ml, 8–9; Carolyn Franks/Shutterstock, 2tl, 10–11; Jeff Greenberg/Getty, 2bl, 12–13; fotografstockholm/iStock, 14–15l; Dave Pot/Shutterstock, 14–15r; Joshua Roper/Alamy, 16.

Library of Congress Cataloging-in-Publication Data
Names: Zimmerman, Adeline J., author.
Title: Apple orchard / by Adeline J. Zimmerman.
Description: Tadpole books edition. | Minneapolis: Jump!, Inc., (2021) | Series: Around town | Includes index. | Audience: Ages 3–6
Identifiers: LCCN 2019047592 (print) | LCCN 2019047593 (ebook) | ISBN 9781645274629 (hardcover) | ISBN 9781645274636 (paperback) | ISBN 9781645274643 (ebook)
Subjects: LCSH: Apples—Juvenile literature. | Orchards—Juvenile literature.
Classification: LCC SB363 .Z56 2021 (print) | LCC SB363 (ebook) | DDC 634/.11—dc23
LC record available at https://lccn.loc.gov/2019047592
LC ebook record available at https://lccn.loc.gov/2019047593

APPLE ORCHARD

by Adeline J. Zimmerman

TABLE OF CONTENTS

tadpole
books

WORDS TO KNOW

basket

orchard

pick

rows

tractor

trees

APPLE ORCHARD

Let's go to the orchard!

We see trees.

They are in rows.

Apples grow on trees.

We pick apples.

basket ·····▶

We fill a basket.

tractor

We go for a tractor ride!

We eat apples.

Yum!

LET'S REVIEW!

What are these people doing at the apple orchard?

INDEX